MW00953022

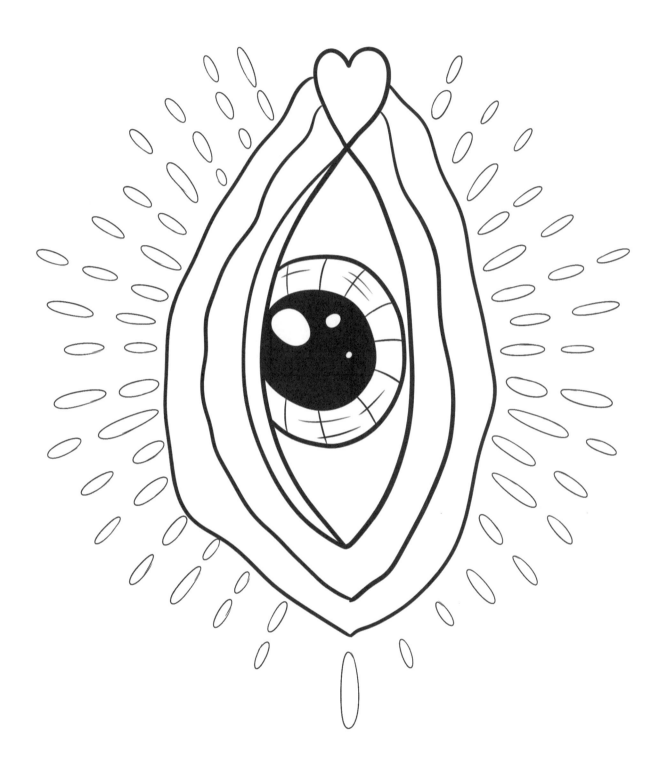

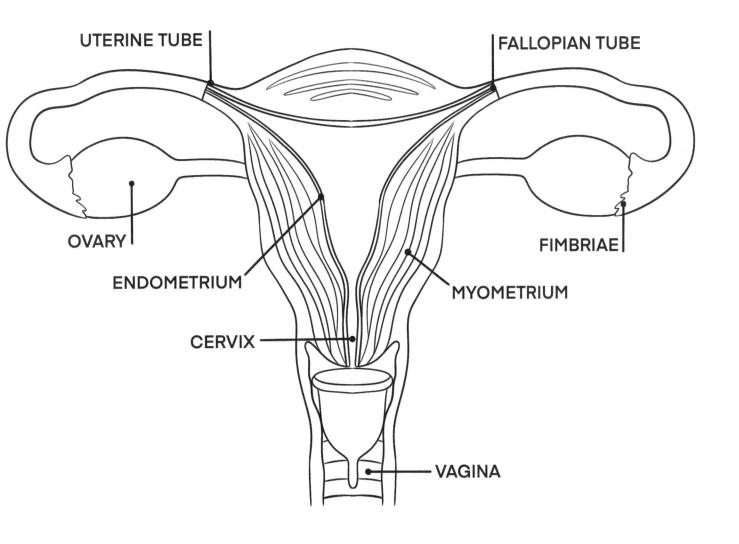

UTERINE TUBE

FALLOPIAN TUBE

OVARY

FIMBRIAE

ENDOMETRIUM

MYOMETRIUM

CERVIX

VAGINA

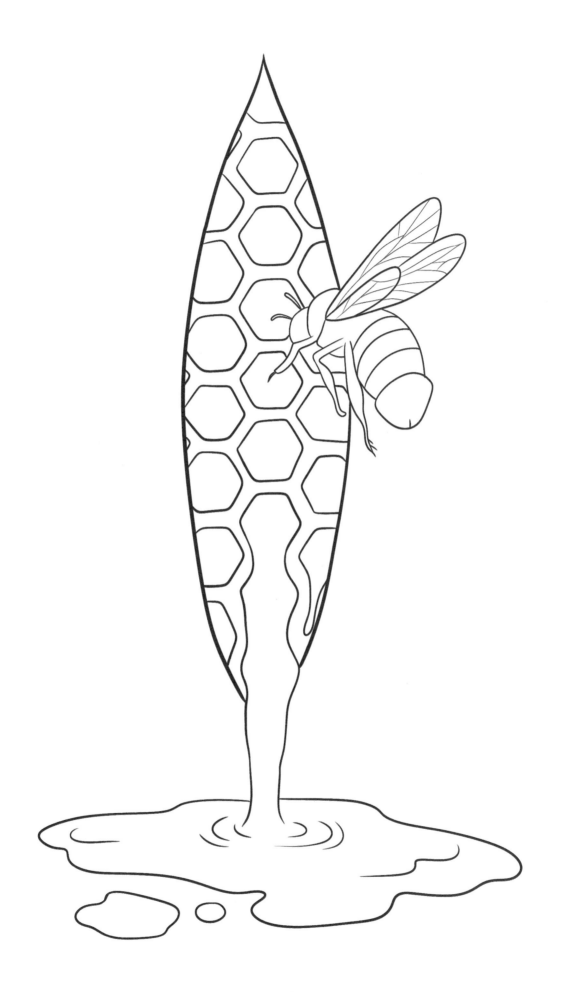

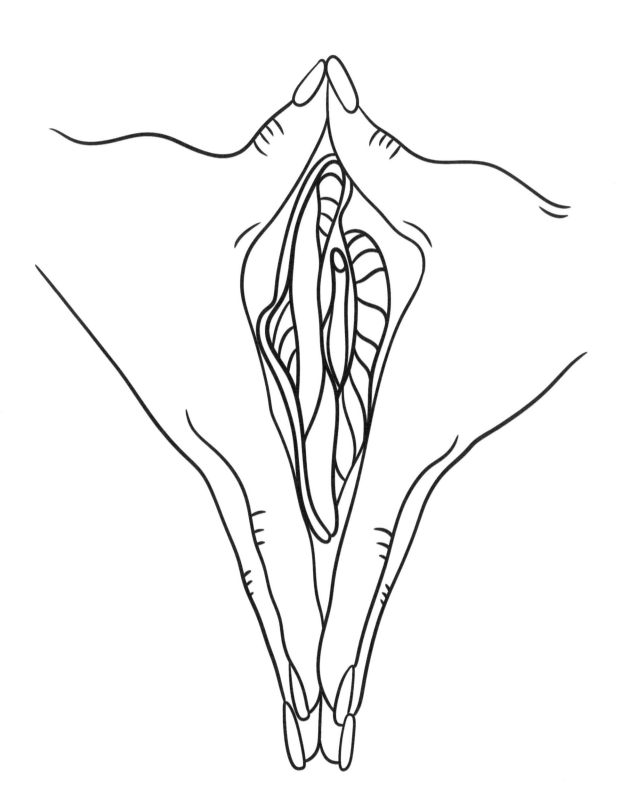

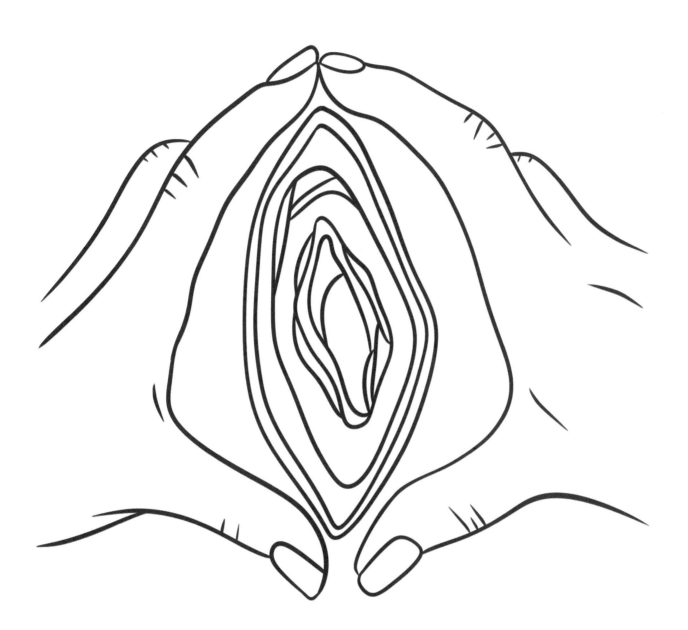

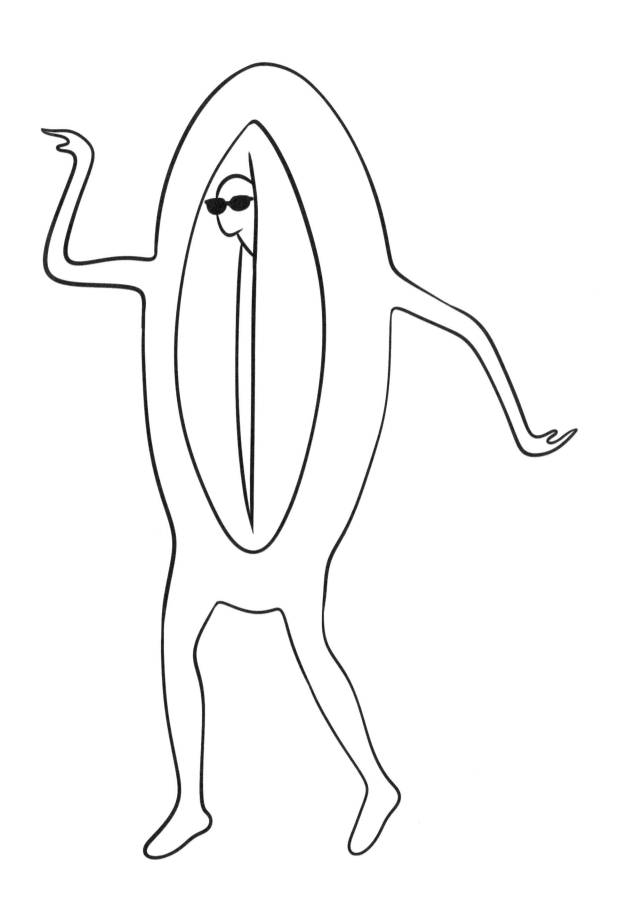

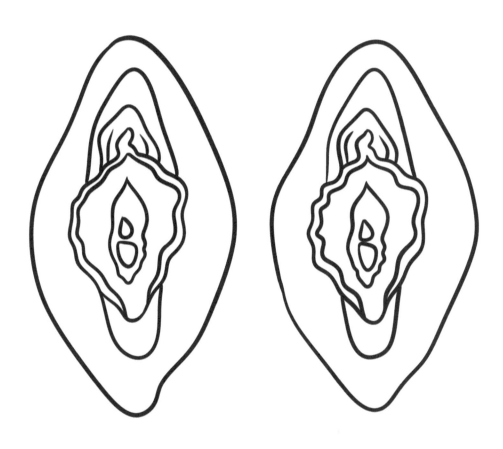

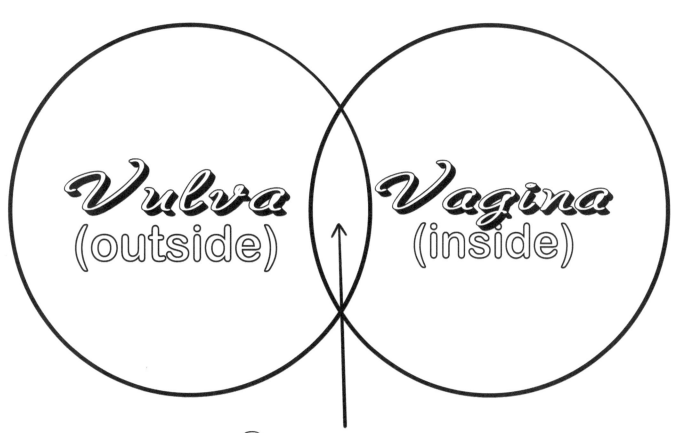

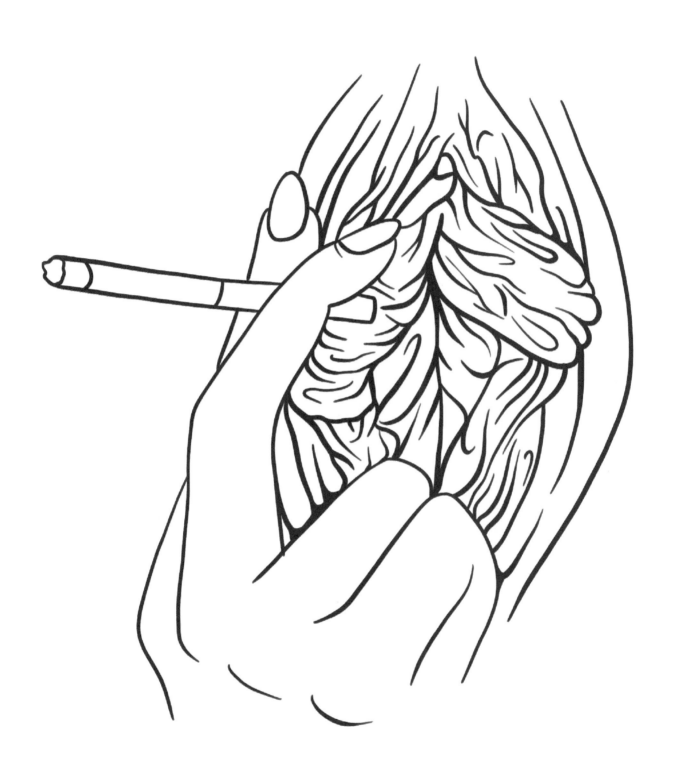

read my lips...

I have the pussy I make the rules

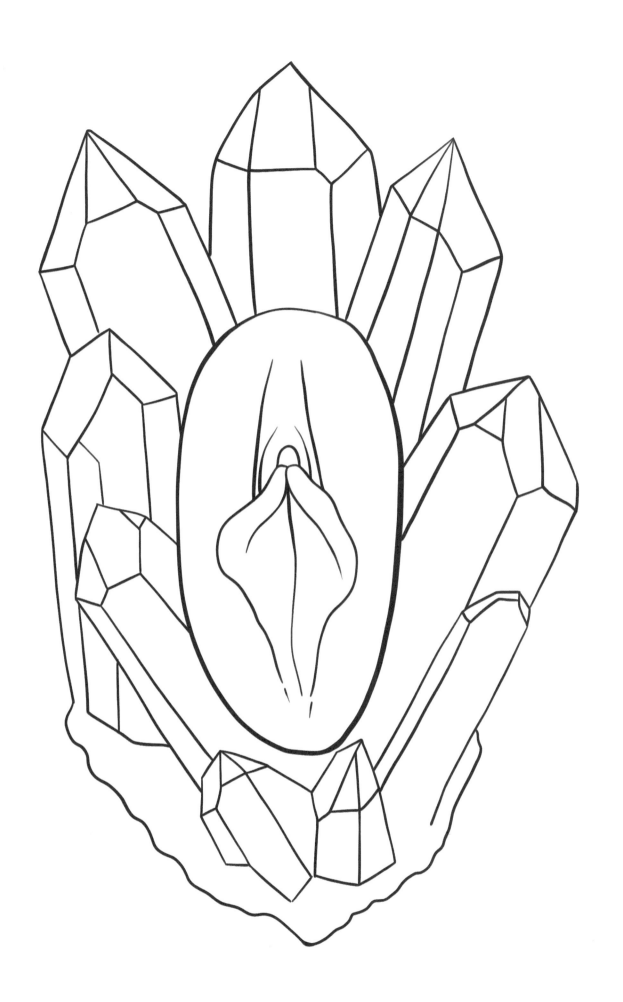

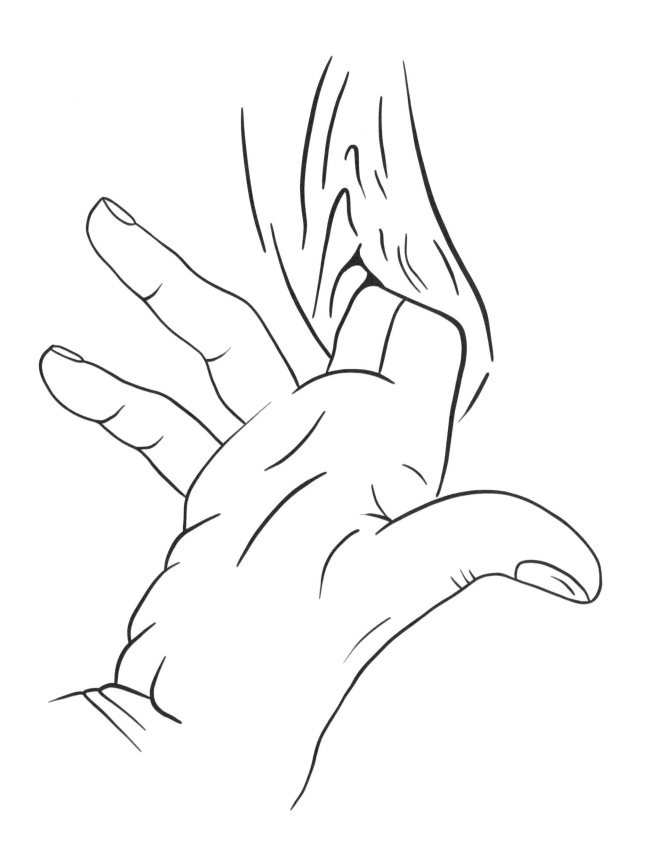

It's
vulva
not
vagina

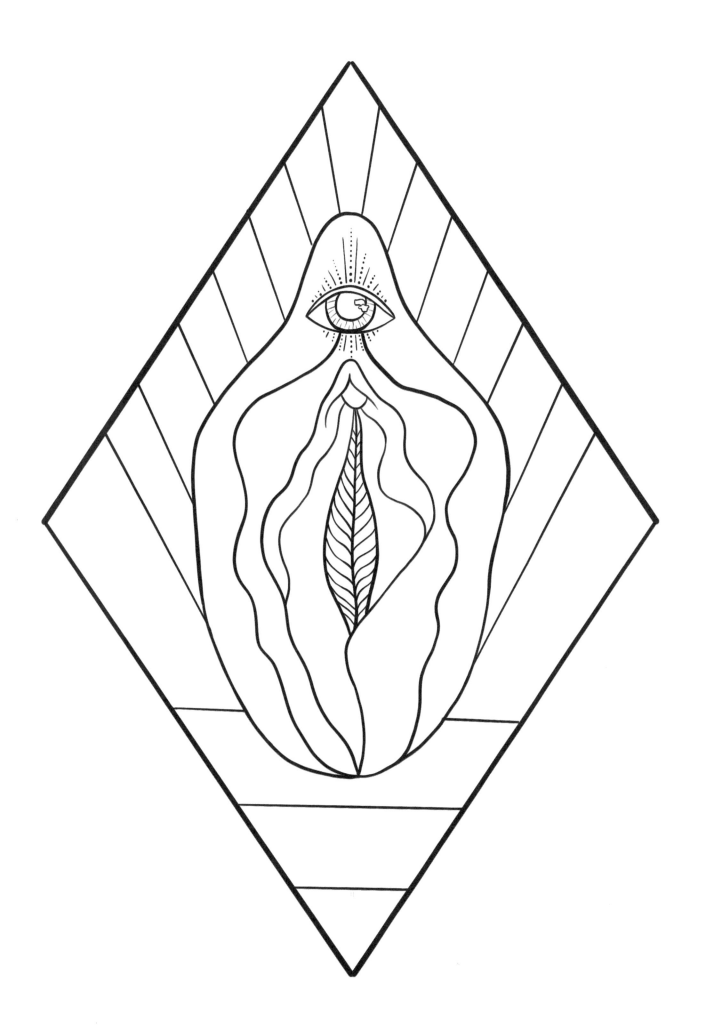

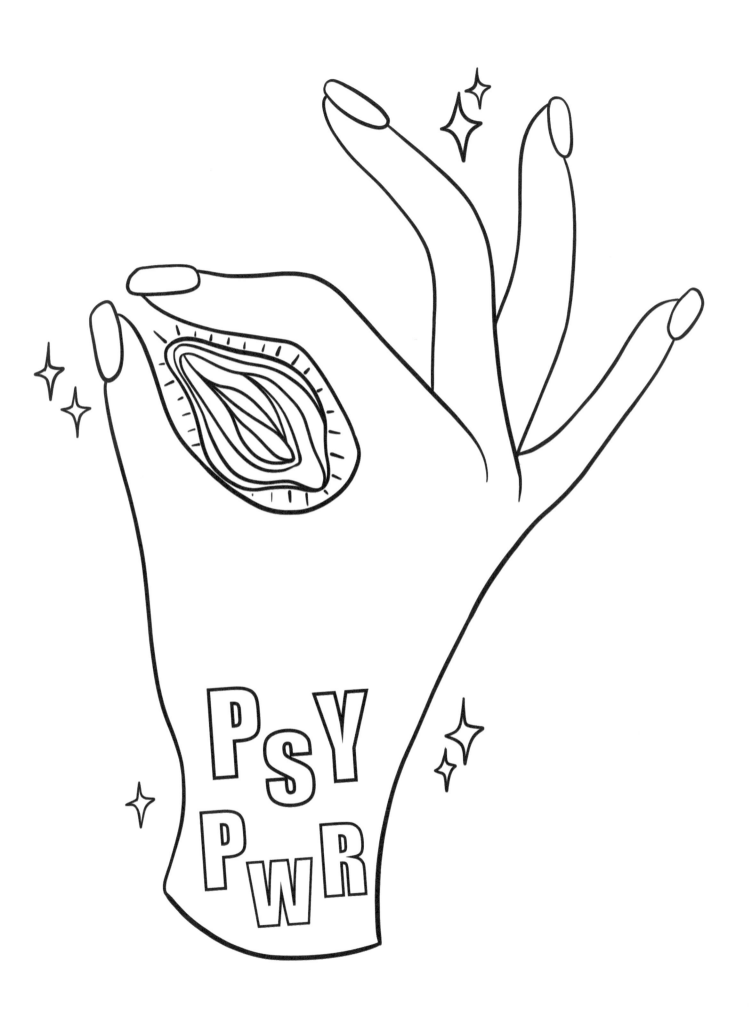

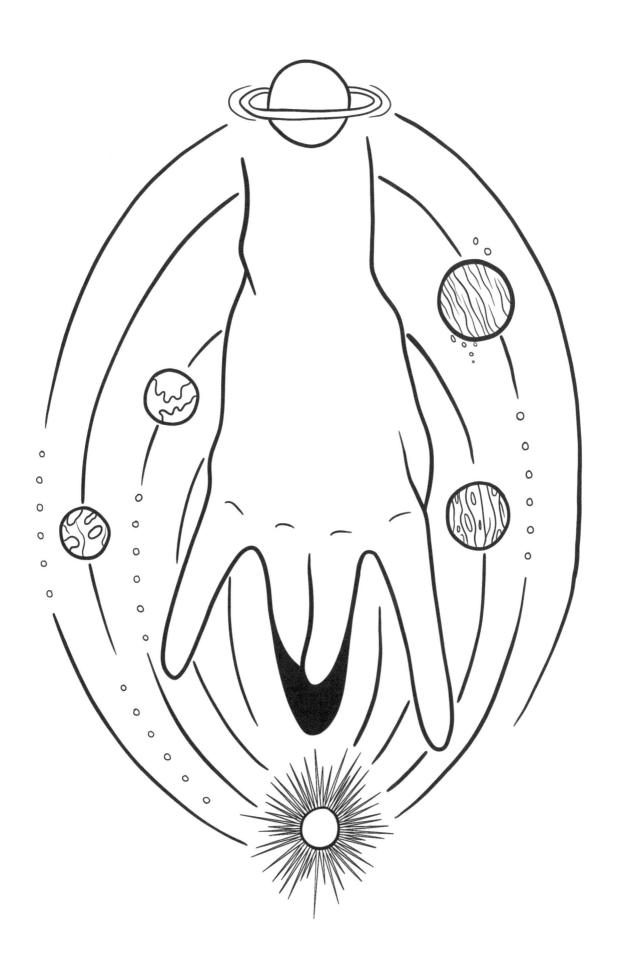

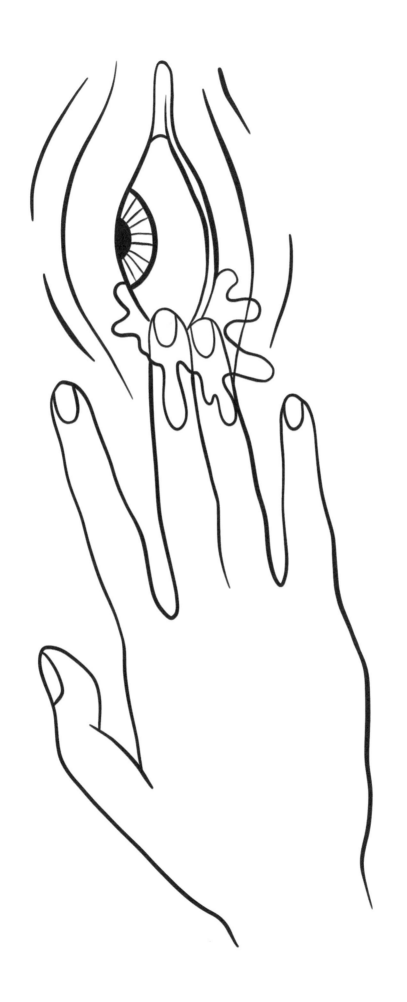

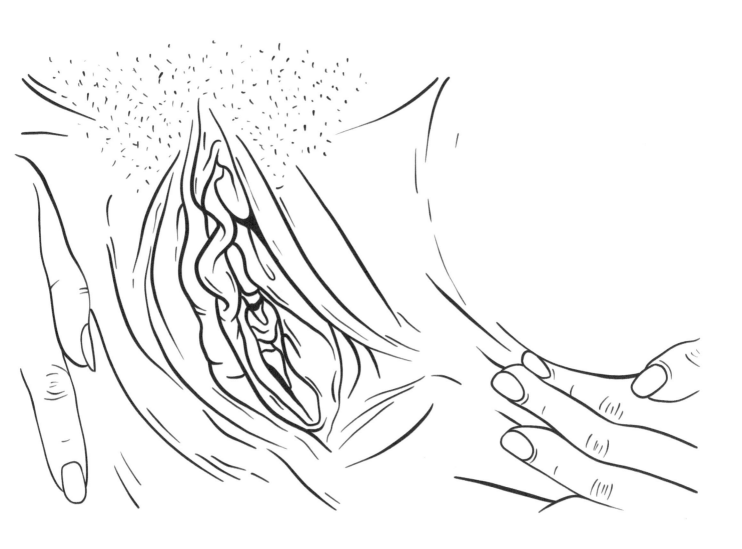

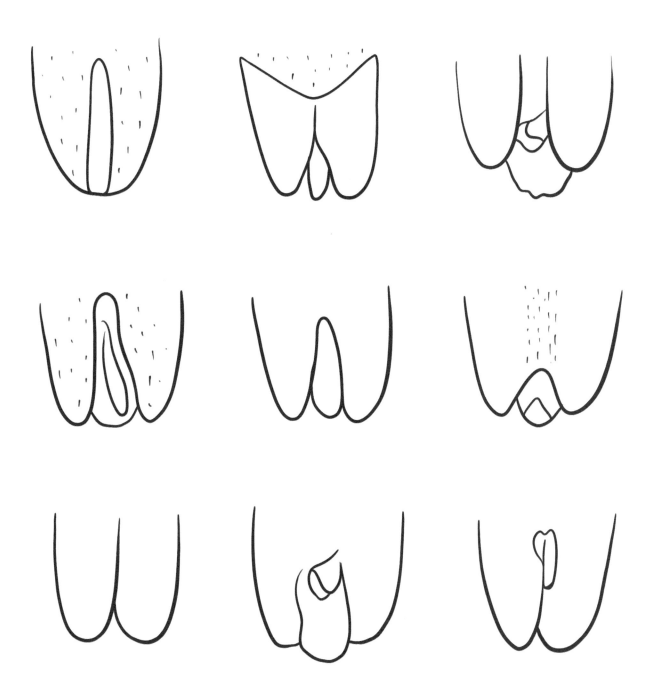

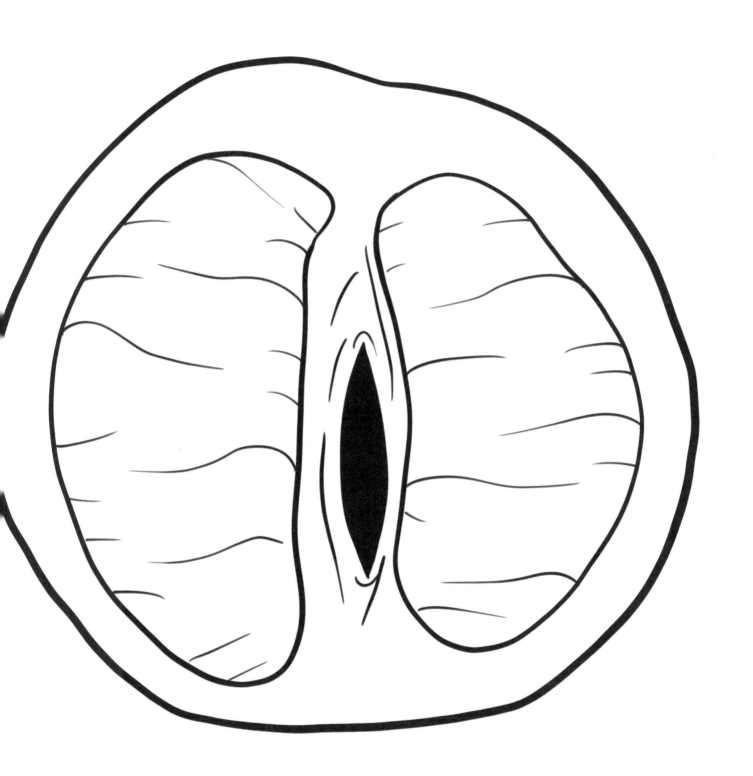

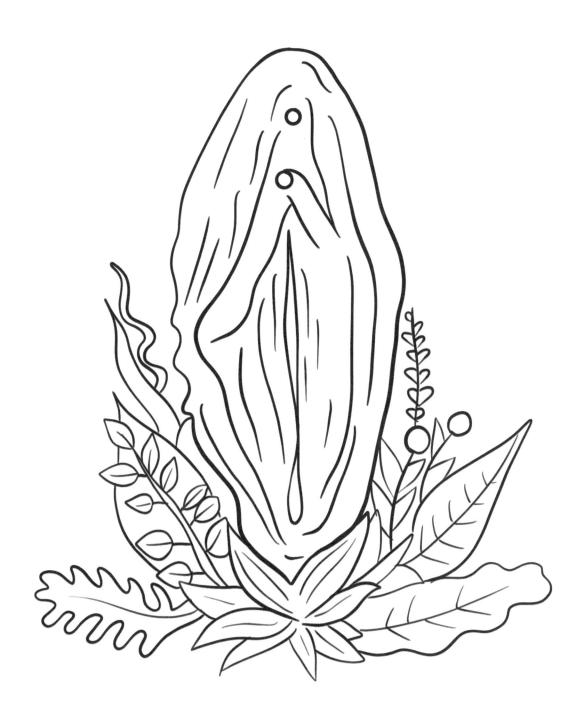

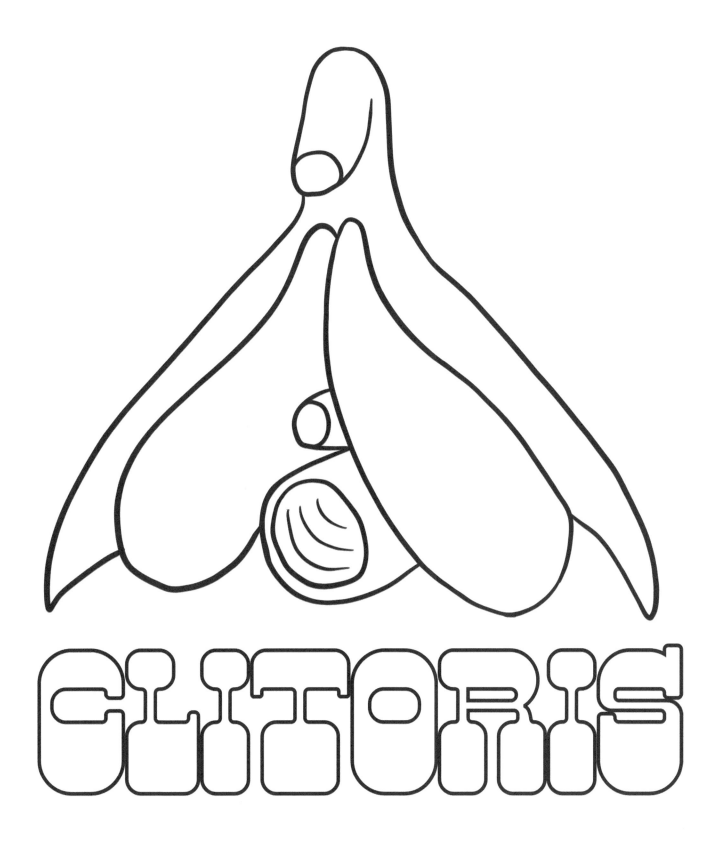

CLITORIS

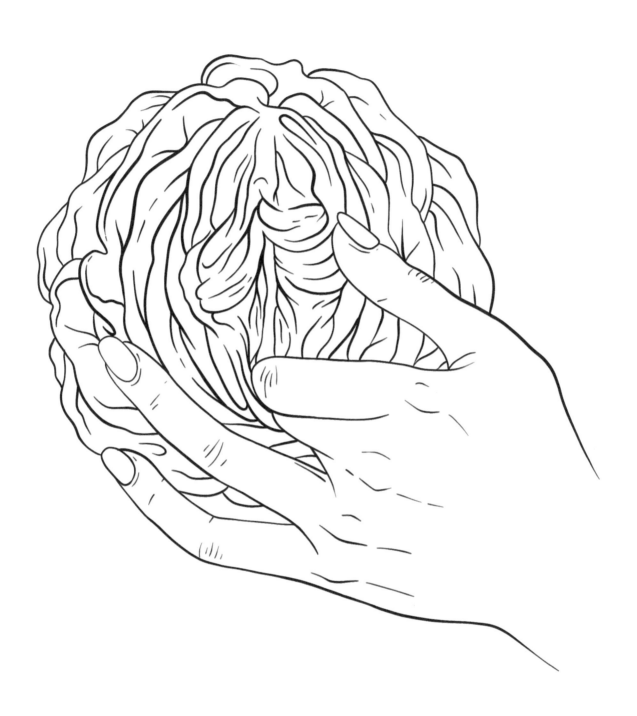

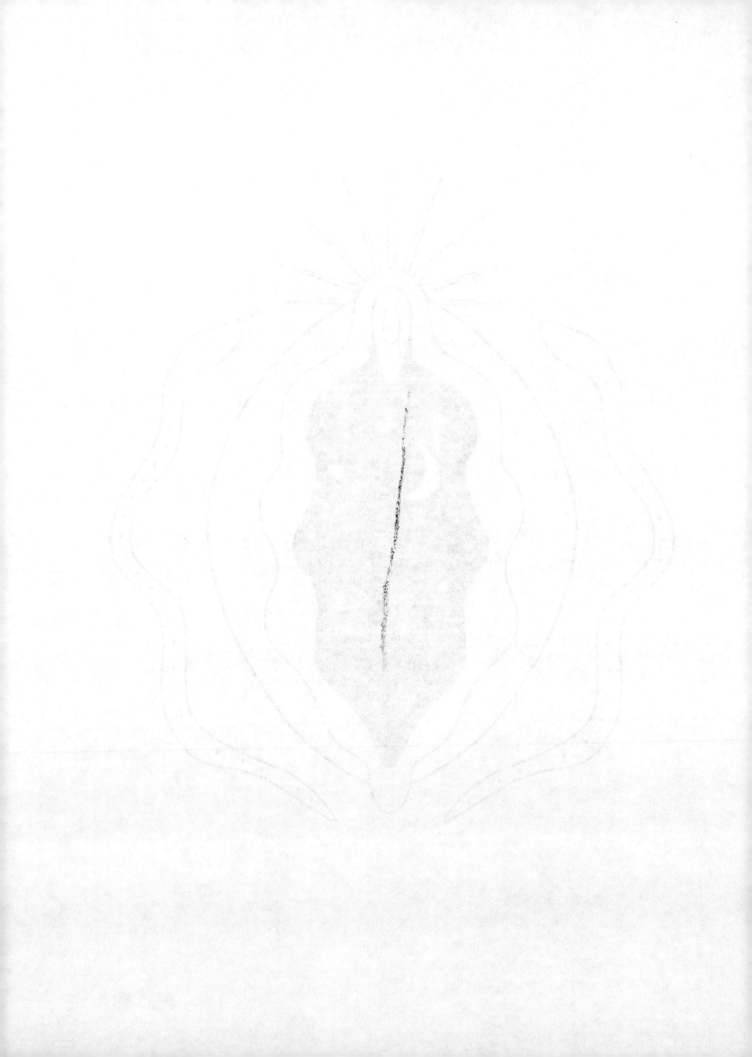

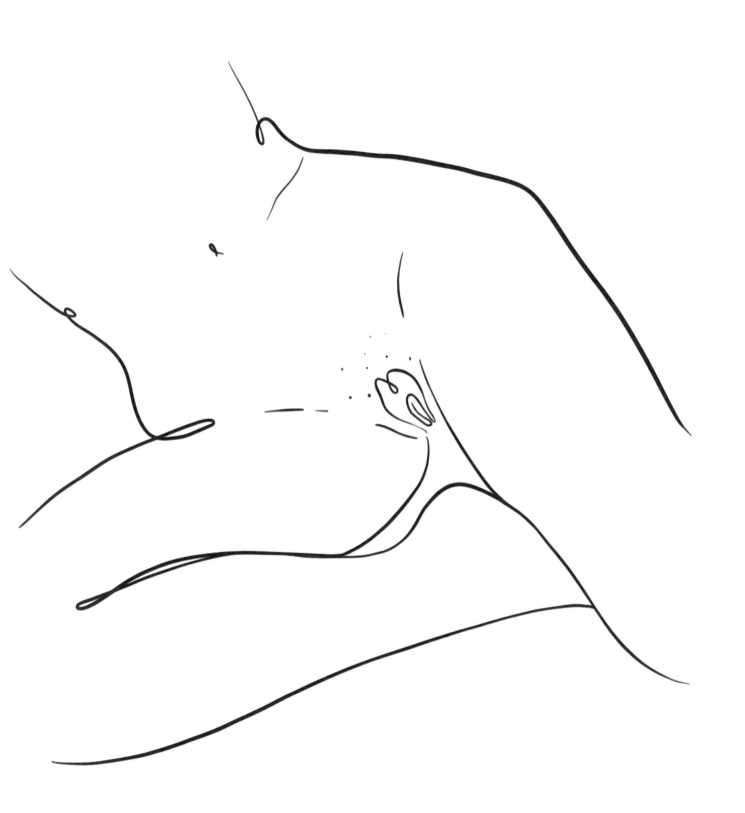

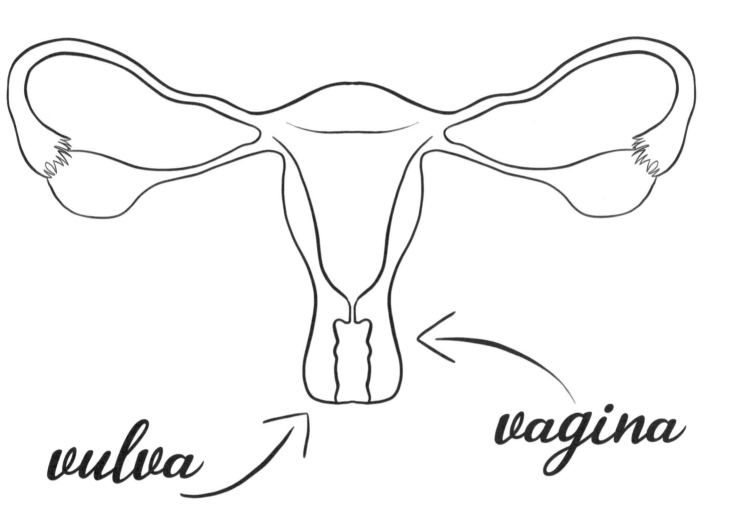

vulva

vagina

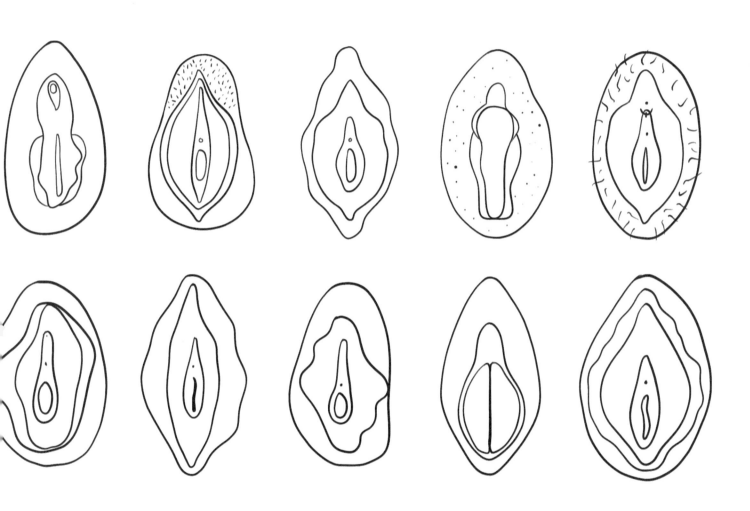

Made in United States
Troutdale, OR
10/21/2024

24023858R00058